A MORAL
BASIS FOR
LIBERTY

A MORAL BASIS FOR LIBERTY

ROBERT SIRICO

Foreword by Edmund A. Opitz

ACTONINSTITUTE

A Moral Basis for Liberty

Reproduced by permission of the Institute of Economic Affairs Health and Welfare Unit, London. Copyright © 1994. Revised Edition, The Foundation for Economic Education, Inc., 1996.

Unless otherwise noted, "Scripture quotations are from The Holy Bible, English Standard Version® (ESV®), copyright © 2001 by Crossway, a publishing ministry of Good News Publishers. Used by permission. All rights reserved."

ISBN 978-1-938948-01-5

British Library Cataloguing in Publication Information Available

Library of Congress Cataloging-in-Publication Data

Sirico, Robert A.

A moral basis for liberty / Robert A. Sirico

ACTON INSTITUTE

98 E. Fulton
Grand Rapids, Michigan 49503
Phone: 616.454.3080
Fax: 616.454.9454
www.acton.org

Printed in the United States of America

CONTENTS

FOREWORD

Edmund A. Opitz

The three key sentences in Father Sirico's finely crafted essay that constitute the theme of this book are: "No civilization in history has survived or flourished without a religious foundation. Nor have great classical liberal thinkers neglected the spiritual dimension of man. From the writings of the late Scholastics to eighteenth-century British economists, they have always discovered a linkage between faith and freedom."

I am honored and privileged to write an introduction to this important work from the skilled pen of an admired friend. What follows is merely a series of reflections inspired by my reading of this slender volume.

The Pilgrims and Puritans who settled along the northeast coast of this country during the seventeenth and eighteenth centuries had sailed across the rugged Atlantic seeking a piece of land where they might put their deepest religious convictions into practice. They were called Dissenters or Separatists; they were estranged from the doctrines and practices of the government church of the nation from which they fled. For their faith, they had suffered various hardships and some persecution. Alexis de Tocqueville, writing of the men and women who established Plymouth Colony observed: "it was a purely intellectual craving that exiled them from the comforts of their former homes; and in facing the inevitable sufferings of exile their object was the triumph of an idea." That idea was conveyed by a motto that Thomas Jefferson used on his personal seal: "Rebellion to tyrants is obedience to God."

These early settlers were not peasants or serfs; they were clergymen and teachers, farmers and men of business. Many had degrees from Cambridge University. The late Samuel Eliot Morison, a Harvard professor specializing in early Massachusetts history, declared that there was a higher percentage of PhDs in the Puritan population in the 1640s than in any time since, in this country.

The idea referred to by Tocqueville had been spreading in England even before the Reformation; it bears directly on the English people having, for the first time, the Bible in their own tongue. The idea of a new commonwealth, fired by reading in the Old Testament of "the people of the covenant," launched in America what Tocqueville described as "a democracy more perfect than antiquity had dared dream of." John Cotton, who has been rightly called the patriarch of New England, served as minister of the First Church of Boston from 1633 until his death in 1653. Cotton Mather wrote that John Cotton "propounded to them an endeavor after a theocracy, as near as might be, to that which was the glory of Israel, the peculiar people.'"

The Puritan regime, taken by itself, might seem to us a pretty rigorous affair, but these people were in what might be termed a fortress-under-siege situation. The first order of business was survival under conditions more primitive than they had experienced in England. Most survived, more people arrived from abroad. They had an educated ministry in every town; they were readers; they had regular news sheets and engaged in vigorous pamphleteering. All towns had a large measure of self-government; they learned about self-government by practicing it in local town meetings. There were, in the pulpits of the time, vigorous and articulate spokesmen for liberty. Here, for instance, is Reverend Daniel Shute of the Second Parish in Hingham, in 1759: "Life, Liberty, and Property are the gifts of the Creator," and again: "Mankind has no right voluntarily to give up to others those natural privileges, essential to their happiness, with which they are invested by the Lord of all; for the improvement of these they are accountable to Him." (I had the privilege of serving in Dr. Shute's pulpit two centuries later.)

The difficulties and dangers of travel in early New England forced each village to generate its own resources. The colonists hunted and fished, grew their own food, and traded with the Indians. Early on, the Pilgrims practiced communal farming by putting all crops into a common warehouse from which all shared. If every member of a community gets an equal share from unequal productivity, it is inevitable that production will slow down. This happened in Plymouth, and the rules were changed. Under the new order each family worked its own plot of land and worked harder knowing that what they produced belonged to them, and it would not be turned over to nonproducers or inefficient workers. As a result, the general level of prosperity rose.

The local churches in New England shared the same creed and were perforce independent of one another; there was no ecclesiastical body to supervise them. A small group of ministers met in Cambridge, Massachusetts, in 1648 and drew up a document that came to be labeled The Cambridge Platform, affirming that the exigencies of the New England situation at the time dictated that each local church must take charge of its own affairs. This polity was called "congregational," and the churches that practiced it were Congregational Churches. This denomination played an important role in American history, not only in New England but also in other parts of the continent as the West was settled.

The early settlers on these shores, whom we have discussed briefly, did not improvise or invent the ideas they brought with them. These people were the heirs of sixteen centuries of cultural, intellectual, and spiritual development of one of the world's great civilizations: the culture called European civilization, or Christendom. There are several other great civilizations, of course, and it is not to disparage them to say that we are the heirs of Western civilization, which is in some ways unique. It is, in the first place, *our* civilization, and American civilization was launched from it as a base.

By the fourth quarter of the eighteenth century, there were thirteen colonies composed of approximately three million people. They were a literate people, knowledgeable in history and apt to quote from Cicero and other Romans but were not fond of Plato with his utopia and its "guardians." They were industrious farmers, merchants, craftsmen, teachers, and writers. Paraphrasing Sir Francis Bacon, they acted on the premise that we work for two reasons: for the glory of God and for the improvement of man's estate. A job was a calling. Adam Smith's *Wealth of Nations* came out in two volumes in 1776 and hundreds of copies were sold in the colonies. No wonder Smith gave his readers a rationale for what they were already doing. He was a free trader; the British were not. The British interfered with trade and treated the colonists as if their main purpose was to give King George some extra income.

The nations of Europe had national churches operating under government funding and control. The colonists had been working toward the idea that churches should be free and independent, and eventually—with the Constitution—the idea became fact. Their way of life demonstrated that the town did not need a government to tell the people what to do; the Bible told them what to do and what not to do. The Commandments forbade murder, theft, false witness, and adultery: The Law is needed to deter those who might wantonly kill a human being and to punish the culprit who has taken another's life. Private property is a sacred trust; the thief who steals what belongs to another, or the arsonist who burns his home, deserves punishment. False witness may be slander or libel; more importantly, it is breach of contract, which is to go back on one's word. "Life, Liberty, and Property" was the popular slogan.

These rules and others come to us in our Bible as the Ten Commandments. They are also engraved into the very nature of things in terms of the way this universe works. General obedience to the Commandments is necessary if we are to have a society, and some society is our natural environment. Only within some society is the full potential of our nature realized.

Imagine a town with a population of ten thousand. Two of its inhabitants are dimwitted and spaced out from time to time. They find life dull so they watch lurid videos and read weird magazines and decide to become Satanists—just the two of them. The town soon learns that it has a couple of "serial killers" in its midst. The town panics after three bodies are found on three successive days. The police are pressured to get tough: gun shops are sold out, houses are double-bolted, alarm systems are installed, and armed vigilante groups are formed spontaneously. Suspicions are rife. The town has ceased being a civic organization and turns into an armed camp—all because a tiny fraction of one percent of its population has turned to murder. We have here a cause-and-effect sequence as convincing as a lab test: This universe has a moral order as an integral part of its natural order, simply awaiting discovery by wise men and seers, and its practice by the rest of us.

The moral order is the natural law, an important concept rooted in Greek and Roman thought, and part of the intellectual equipment of European thinkers until recent times. It was a central element in the legal philosophy of our Founding Fathers. It was also referred to as the higher law, and as such is part of the title of Edwin Corwin's important little book of some sixty years ago,

The "Higher Law" Background of American Constitutional Theory.
Positive law, in contrast to the natural law, is the kind of law
enacted by legislators, or decreed by commissions. Natural law
is discovered. Positive law is good law if it accords with natural
law but becomes bad law if it runs counter to natural law.

The Founding Fathers appealed to natural law argument in
their attacks on restrictive legislation that impaired their rightful liberties. Jefferson declared that God had made the mind of
man free, implying that any interference with men's peaceable
actions, or any subordination of one man to another is bad law;
it violates the fundamental intent of nature and nature's God.

Thus they conceived the idea of a separation of powers in
government—executive, legislative, and judicial—plus a retention
of certain prerogatives in the several states. This was the purpose
of the remarkable group of men who met to forge an instrumen-
tality of government in conformity with the natural law, based
on the widely held conviction that God is the author of liberty.
In short, our political liberties were not born in a vacuum; they
emerged among a people who believed in their unique destiny
under God—the God whose nature, works, and demands they
gleaned from the Old and New Testaments. The eighteenth-
century New England clergymen were learned men and often
spoke along these lines. Many sermons made their way into print
and Liberty Press has favored us with a mammoth one-volume
collection of them. Such messages contributed much to the mental
climate of the time, which Jefferson and his committee drew
upon to compose the immortal words that give our Declaration
of Independence its enduring influence.

The Declaration is the first of the documents upon which this
nation was founded, the others being the Articles of Confed-
eration, the Constitution, and the Northwest Ordinance.

Let us examine the opening words of the Declaration: "*We* hold
these truths to be self-evident...." The Declaration did not say
that "these truths *are* self-evident," or that *all men* hold them to

be such. This is not true. Were it possible for us to cross-examine the "We" who offered the Declaration, they might explain that "We" are speaking, first, for those of us here gathered; and second, for the generality of our fellows whom we judge to share our view as determined by the clergy they admire, the pamphlets they write and circulate, the Committees of Correspondence, and the documents emanating from the legislators of the thirteen colonies. "We" are the end result of long exposure to the Bible, which teaches us that we are created beings and not the accidental end result of a chance encounter of atoms; and that we belong on this planet, earth, which was created to teach us what we need to know in order to grow, train our characters, and become the mature men and women we have it in us to be. God has given us reason and free will, which we often misuse so as to cause a breach between God and ourselves, and for our sins Christ died on the cross—not just for some of us but for all of us. It is in this sense that "all men are created equal," male and female, master and bondsman. They are unequal and different in other respects, as common observation convinces us. Richard Rumbold, convicted in England because of his beliefs, ascended the scaffold in 1685 and uttered these immortal words: "none comes into the world with a saddle on his back; neither does one come booted and spurred to ride him." Jefferson quoted these words in one of his letters; it is a fair surmise that they had an effect on his own thinking and writing.

A group of extraordinary men assembled in Philadelphia and gave us a Constitution. In 1789, after much debate, it was accepted by the required number of states, and the United States of America took its place among the nations of the world.

While the Constitution was being debated and argued out, 1787–1789, three very able public men who were also philosophers—James Madison, John Jay, and Alexander Hamilton—presented the case for adoption in the public press, eighty-five essays in all. The essays were gathered in book form as *The Federalist* (or sometimes *The Federalist Papers*), which has long assumed its place as a major work of political philosophy, certainly the finest exposition of the nature and requirements of a republican form of government. It is an indispensable treatise and rationale for the governmental structures essential to equal freedom in a civilized social order, as envisioned by the men we refer to as the Founding Fathers. My suspicion is that in today's colleges few political science majors are exposed to it.

The Declaration opens with a theological statement, asserting that our rights are Creator-endowed. This plants the idea of a political order rooted in the Transcendent, designed to maximize individual liberty in society, and incorporating the great "thou shalt nots" of the Ten Commandments. The citizens were already earning their daily bread by working along free-market economy lines even before they discovered *The Wealth of Nations*; thus our threefold society: religious-moral, legal-political, and economic-commercial. These three sectors interact and mutually implicate one another, supporting one another as well.

People tend to act out their beliefs, and our characters are shaped by our deepest and most firmly held convictions. As we believe so will we become; as we are so will our societies be. The religious, moral, and political convictions of our late eighteenth-century forebears were not improvised on the spot. They were supported by eighteen centuries of Western experience in religious, ethical, and political matters. History has had its ups and downs and its gigantic swings, and some historians find major changes about every five hundred years from the beginning of the Christian era. The modern age might find its pivotal point at the time of the Renaissance, Reformation, and Counter-Reformation. Christendom was sharply divided; minor sects proliferated. It was a time of exploration; the West came to realize that there were other civilizations with religions of their own that were far more ancient than Christendom, including sacred scriptures. A few Western philosophers began to realize that there is no reason why the God they believed in—the God of the Bible—should limit his attention to one narrow part of the world, and a relative newcomer on the world scene at that. We do have something to learn from Islam, Buddhism, and Hinduism, as well as from Taoism and Confucianism. They, too, have much to learn from us, but that is another story.

Most of us do not create the ideas and assumptions that guide our everyday actions. We borrow from thinkers of the past whose names we may not know. Joseph Wood Krutch taught at Columbia University and was a well-known drama critic with the mind of a philosopher. Here is his thumbnail description of how the modern mind was formed, the assumptions we habitually act upon:

> The fundamental answers which we have on the whole made, and which we continue to accept, were first given in the seventeenth century by Francis Bacon, Thomas Hobbes, and René Descartes, and were later elaborated by Marx and the Darwinians.

He lists these items in chronological order:

1. The most important task to which the human mind may devote itself is the "control of nature" through technology. Knowledge is power (Bacon, 1561–1626).

2. Man may be completely understood if he is considered to be an animal, making predictable reactions to that desire for pleasure and power to which all his other desires may, by analysis, be reduced (Hobbes, 1588–1679).

3. All animals, man excepted, are pure machines (Descartes, 1596–1650).

4. Man, Descartes notwithstanding, is also an animal and therefore also a machine (Darwin, 1809–1882).

5. The human condition is not determined by philosophy, religion, or moral ideas because all of these are actually only by-products of social and technological developments which take place independent of man's will and uninfluenced by the "ideologies" they generate (Marx, 1818–1883).

These observations are tendentious, of course, but there does seem to be a warped streak in the philosophies of the past four or five centuries as they wander away from common sense. An observation from University of Glasgow professor C. A. Campbell seems pertinent: As history amply testifies, it is from powerful, original, and ingenious thinkers that the queerest aberrations of philosophic theory often emanate. Indeed it may be said to require a thinker exceptionally endowed in these respects if the more paradoxical type of theory is to be expounded in a way that will make it seem tenable even to its authors—let alone to the general public.

Some modern philosophers seem to have given up on man, and even distrust their own reason. Here is the brilliant Bertrand Russell, for example, from his celebrated essay entitled *Free Mans Worship*, "Man," he writes, "is the product of causes which had no prevision of the end they were achieving; his origin, his growth, his hopes and fears, his loves and his beliefs, are but the outcome of accidental collocations of atoms." Russell has just stated one of his beliefs that, on his own showing, is the result of an accidental coming together of some atoms, to which the categories true and false do not apply. He continues: "Brief and powerless is mans life; on him and all his race the slow, sure doom falls pitiless and dark. Blind to good and evil, reckless of destruction, omnipotent matter rolls on its relentless way." Matter is simply inert, until the mind of some human decides to use it to further some human purpose. Omnipotent, indeed! To Russell's credit he does admit that "good" is real and so is "evil." Obviously, we cannot be blind to that which is not there.

Russell not only has done brilliant work in mathematics but also in the philosophy of science. However, if man is in such a sorry state as Russell thinks, then ordinary humans need a keeper. Enter the humanitarian with a guillotine. Actually, the record shows that human beings play a variety of roles, both good and evil. We know the horrors of twentieth-century totalitarianism and collectivism, and we also know the glories of Periclean Athens, Florence at its peak, Elizabethan England, and the late eighteenth-century colonists who laid down the political structures of a free society. Nearly every person has untapped skills and strengths, drawn upon only when urgently needed. We needed them in the 1780s and 1790s, and they gave us the legal framework for a market economy. The market operated here more freely than ever before—or since. There were government interventions all the way along, of course, increasing after the Civil War. Even then the market was so open and free that, of the thirty million immigrants who came to these shores during the last three decades of the nineteenth century, nearly every one got a job. Looking back, we would be shocked by some of the working conditions. The workers, however, compared their present employment to much worse conditions in the old country. Here, at least, they could work their way up the ladder and they were confident that their children would fare better than they.

In aristocratic England, rural poverty did not attract much attention, but when these poor folk flocked into the cities, poverty became a concern of many well-intentioned folk. We know something of the slum scene in mid-eighteenth-century London as depicted in William Hogarth's drawings. Things were not much better a hundred and fifty years later, according to Jack London, who spent some time exploring slum life in London and wrote up his findings in his *People of the Abyss*. There is something of a novelist's embellishments in the book but there is no doubt that many men, women, and children lived miserably. What is the cause of poverty, and what is the remedy?

A poor society is one saddled with low productivity, and low productivity means a low ratio of capital to labor—that is, few tools and little machinery. Poverty has been the fate of most people who have ever lived on this earth. We began to move in the direction of prosperity when people in our section of the planet began to till their own plots of land and then enjoy the full fruits of their labor. Human ingenuity was turned loose, resulting in more and better tools provided by increasingly skilled workers in various crafts. The concept of private property was redefined and people began to trade more freely.

A few men had speculated about economics before Adam Smith, but he made of it a new science, inspiring scholars for the next two centuries. We now know how to create the conditions for optimum economic well-being. It is now possible to have a free and prosperous commonwealth. First, operate within the political order envisioned by the Declaration of Independence and the Constitution; this gives us the Rule of Law—one law for all persons alike because we are one in our essential humanness. Second, put into practice the truths of economics gleaned from the classic treatises from Adam Smith to Ludwig von Mises and other scholars of today Third, there is the moral factor. We have in our time suffered from loss of touch with the transcendent aspect of human experience, although we are intimately involved with it, in the case of our own minds. The mind transcends the body, but they interact with one another. The mind-body problem is as ancient as philosophy. We know that they interact although how they interact is something of a puzzle. The body is an object in space and time, compounded of the common chemicals found in the earth's crust. The body can be weighed and measured; it can be looked at and touched, but the mind has no such characteristics. It is immaterial but it can affect the material body, guide its actions, generate certain illnesses, or enhance its wellness.

Your mind transcends your body, yet is also acting in it and with it. Analogously, it might be suggested that God, conceived as Spirit, transcends this universe and yet is immanent within it. This is a mystery, of course, but hardly more of a mystery than how your mind interacts with your body. From this perspective the idea of the natural law or the moral order as a real part of this mysterious universe falls into place.

A new religion emerged in the West during the nineteenth century to challenge Christianity: socialism. This is a pseudo-religion, but, during the first several decades of the nineteenth century, it aroused a moral fervor comparable to that of the early Christians. In 1848, Charles Kingsley and F. D. Maurice, two clergymen from the Church of England, launched a movement called Christian Socialism. Their aim was to vindicate for "the Kingdom of Christ" its "true authority over the realms of industry and trade," and "for socialism its true character as the great Christian revolution of the 19th century."

The year 1848 also saw publication of *The Communist Manifesto*, which referred to its socialist rival in derisive terms: "Christian Socialism is but the holy water with which the priest consecrates the heartburnings of the aristocrat."

The movement spread in England, and into the United States where its common name was the Social Gospel. A popular slogan was: "Christianity is the religion of which Socialism is the practice." Well-known theologians contended that, "To be a Christian and not a Socialist, is to be guilty of heresy!"

Socialists of all stripes have, from the beginning, spoken as if they had a monopoly of all the virtues; only socialists strive for justice in society, peace between nations, and help for the poor. As a matter in fact, all men and women of good will want to see other people better off; better fed, clothed, and housed; better educated; healthier and benefiting from skilled medical care; and peace among the nations and just relations within the nation.

Socialists would endorse these goals, to which they would add a utopian vision, but the means the socialist employs is at odds with his goals. The socialist would structure his society along the lines of a chain of command all the way to the masses at the bottom. The operational imperatives of a socialistic society cancel out the socialist dream. No society organized socialistically has been able to provide sufficient goods and services to raise its masses above the poverty level, and the citizenry are not free men and women. For a century and a half, it was a religion that dominated the lives of millions; it is now revealed as a "religion" whose god has failed. The failure of this false deity offers us a clue: Turn in the opposite direction to find the true God and his moral order.

Not all proponents of the free-market economy, private-property order are theists, and they do have a concern for an ethic compatible with capitalism, referring to "enlightened self-interest" as the guide to right conduct. This is not a sound theory, in my view, nor is it an accurate reading of the ethic appropriate to a capitalist economy.

Enlightened self-interest as a moral principle has its advocates, but it exhibits some logical difficulties. The term has no referent, or else it has as many referents as there are selves, and each self's interest may differ from day to day. Continuity is lacking because no enduring principle can be deduced from any multiple of private inclinations. Furthermore, if a person is urged to pursue his own interest, he cannot be denied the right to decide what that interest is. Therefore, if A is allowed to decide for B what B's self-interest is then B will be acting out A's interest and not his own. There is no norm or standard transcending both A and B by which we might be able to determine who might be right and who wrong.

Thus, "do your own thing" is the rule, and the weak who do their thing are at the mercy of the strong who do theirs. The clever and unscrupulous who do their thing have the rest of us at a disadvantage. If every individual merely pursues his own interest or pursues his private advantage, it is impossible from this starting point to arrive at any sort of a general rule or principle or ethical norm. Mr. B might *call* something a norm or principle, but only because his self-interest dictates that he do so. If there are no moral rules, why should Mr. B, having been told to pursue self-interest, refrain from fraud or theft or aggression when his self-interested calculation of costs and benefits determines that the benefits accruing to him outweigh the costs? When all is said and done, there is no substitute for the time-tested code built into the nature of things, whose mandates form the necessary foundation of a good society: Do not murder. Do not steal. Do not assault. Keep your word. Fulfill your contracts.

Furthermore, the self-interest ethic does not represent an accurate rendering of the capitalist ethos, although most defenders of capitalism have adopted it. In the market economy the consumers' needs, wants, and desires are sovereign; entrepreneurs wishing to maximize profits obediently accept the dictates of the market. No one is forced to become an entrepreneur, but if he does assume that role he must subordinate his own desires to the demands of his customers.

Let Ludwig von Mises show just how much self-abnegation the entrepreneur must practice. "In the market society," he writes,

> the proprietors of capital and land can enjoy their property only by employing it for the satisfaction of other people's wants. They must serve the consumers in order to have any advantage from what is their own. The very fact that they own means of production forces them to submit to the wishes of the public. Ownership is an asset only for those who know how to employ it in the best possible way for the benefit of the consumers. It is a social function." (*Human Action*, 684)

Mises also said:

> For in an unhampered market society the consumers daily decide anew who should own and how much he should own. The consumers allot control of the means of production to those who know how to use them best for the satisfaction of the most urgent wants of the consumers.... [The owners], ... are mandataries of the consumers, bound by the operation of the market to serve the consumers best." (683)

Such is the free-market extension of the Good Samaritan ethic, to which one can only say, "Amen."

A MORAL BASIS FOR LIBERTY

Robert A. Sirico

Summary

A secure liberty is based on a firm moral foundation, but the moral terminology of contemporary political debate is often secretly at war with liberty. This represents more than linguistic confusion; it represents a danger to the proper exercise of virtue in the context of freedom. While liberty's historical roots are found in the Jewish and Christian religions, the moral principles of both are overlooked in modern discussion of such basic institutions as entrepreneurship and the welfare state. Modern discussion and evaluation of the two institutions are in need of radical correction. Advocates of capitalism and economic liberty can and should assume the moral high ground.

Introduction

In his widely discussed treatise *The End of History and the Last Man*,[1] Francis Fukuyama argues that democratic capitalism has no serious competitor remaining in the struggle over the most desirable organizational principle of society, economy, and politics. What is left to us in the rest of the decade and the next century, he suggests, falls largely under the rubrics of management: improving the administration of public policy, debating spending priorities, fine-tuning regulations, and sustaining an appropriate mix of liberty and equality that satisfies the most urgent demands of both. The big battles over ideology are over, Fukuyama argues.

Few would dispute that events of the last few years have shown the practical desirability of markets over socialism, and in this, the "end of history" thesis seems correct. Yet there is good reason to doubt that this victory is total. Despite the efforts of many great economists, political philosophers, and historians, economic liberty is far from having captured the moral high ground in public debate. If economic liberty is valued, it is rarely because it is considered more just or more proper than any alternative. It is too often valued solely on the kinds of managerial and technical grounds Fukuyama suggests will consume our efforts in the post-Cold War world.

We feel free to argue about how many "jobs" this or that piece of legislation creates, but we are squeamish about asking whose property will be used to create these jobs, or whether it is better to have property commandeered by political authority or put to voluntary use by market participants. An argument over whether there ought to be ceilings on corporate remuneration centers on whether high salaries are economically justifiable, and not on whether government ought to have say over such matters in the first place. We might dispute a proposal to force private

---

[1] Francis Fukuyama, *The End of History and the Last Man* (New York: Free Press, 1992).

business to add another function to its list of mandated benefits on grounds of cost, but not on grounds of the right and wrong uses of private enterprise.

Consider the opinions of men and women whose work affords opportunity for philosophical reflection on morality—the two most prominent being academics and ecclesiastics. How many among them can offer—or would even be willing to try—a moral defense of private property and free markets? A safe answer is precious few. How can the institutions of liberty survive and flourish so long as the moral opinion-makers are so overwhelmingly sympathetic to only one side of the debate?

The triumph of the managerial techniques of statecraft over authentic reflection on the moral principles of economics is only a small part of the broader decline of religion. In what some have called the new age of paganism, the culture has less and less respect for transcendent norms. It follows that with this decline would come an overvaluation of the potential for human reason alone to guide us. A secularist state of mind exalts skill above faith, technique above prayer, the practical above the principled, relativism above standards of truth.

It is my contention that the loss of a normative defense of liberty introduces a certain instability to the social order. The efficiency defense of economic liberty is not enough, and management of a truly free society without reference to the natural law will ultimately prove injurious to liberty itself. So long as economic liberty—and its requisite institutions of private property, free exchange, capital accumulation, and contract enforcement—is not backed by a generally held set of norms by which it can be defended, it cannot be sustained over the long term. Into the moral vacuum left by capitalism's defenders rush notions hostile to economic liberty, notions drawn largely from the values and vocabularies of interventionism and socialism.

Further, if a principled defense of markets based on the principle of private property and the virtue of voluntarism is absent from public life, it is very likely that the moral center of the buying public has begun to slip as well. In any market, the kinds of goods and services producers provide reflect the values of the consuming public. That is both the virtue and the vice of the consumer sovereignty inherent in market transactions where the consumer is king. Where the values of the buying public are disordered, the products available in the market will be disordered as well. Where a free people's actions and preferences are informed by spiritual concerns, market activity and wealth accumulation present no danger in themselves. As the economist Wilhelm Roepke argued, institutional virtue and public virtue are codependent.[2]

Societies that have a deep and unyielding respect for the principle of private property have traditionally fostered institutions that we associate with a vibrant social and cultural life—for example, intact families, savings and deferred gratification, cooperative social norms, and the morality of natural law. Similarly, cultural decadence, family collapse, and widespread secularization have corresponded with statism and socialism more times than an essay of this length could name. The link is more than suggestive; it is direct. Economic liberty needs a moral defense.

The Linguistic Boundaries of Debate

Many of the confusions of our age rest on a loss of certain crucial distinctions. The most apparent is the distinction between rights and privileges. John Hospers, my philosophy professor at the University of Southern California, used to say we have undergone a "rights inflation." As in a monetary inflation, the value of the common unit of measurement has been drastically watered down. For all the talk about rights, we lack a clear understanding of what constitutes meaningful rights.

---

2 Wilhelm Roepke, *The Humane Economy* (South Bend, IN: Gateway, 1960).

Rights are the claims that the individual has against others. An example is the right to life, which is another way of saying any one person has a just claim not to be injured by another. Rights represent more than a legal claim. In order for rights to be inalienable, as Jefferson proclaimed them to be, rights must exist prior to and independent of any legal or institutional rules, such as the Bill of Rights. Laws and institutions may obfuscate, violate, or protect an individual's rights, but they can neither grant nor remove rights. Rights, in order to be claims that are inalienable and fundamental, must exist independent of the coercive apparatus of the state. In order for rights to be all that we have just said, they must derive from the nature of the case, which is to say, the human person must possess rights by virtue of his or her very nature.

Many of today's so-called rights have nothing to do with this older idea. Most often they are the consequence of the political process, as if legislators and civil servants are capable of conferring immutable claims on groups. We may speak, for example, of the right to cosmetic surgery on demand at a low price. If we assert this right, we are implicitly denying the long-accepted right to the security of private property one has in one's just earnings, that they not be taken by others through force. The payment of cosmetic services rendered at a low price must be fulfilled by taking the property holdings of members of the general public. It is a right that contradicts other rights and thus cannot be considered a "natural" right, one that flows from our nature as acting human persons.

Another basic distinction I wish to draw is that which exists between a community or a society and a government or political order. A society may exist with or without a particular political arrangement. The Philippine society continued to exist despite the deposition of the Marcos political regime. Even a regime as brutal as that of Soviet Russia left behind a Russian society that has a legitimate claim to continuity with the pre-Soviet one. Similarly, a community is distinct in that its members hold certain values, mores, customs, and culture in common, but it is not marked by legal recognition or coercive capacity. Yet today the term *community* is often used to put a humanitarian gloss on what used to be called a political pressure group.

We can make a further distinction between community and collective. People can enjoy a life in common, sharing values, homes, property, and philosophy in common without the requirement that it be held together by force or the threat of force. Collectives are something different in this taxonomy because they require coercion to enact and sustain. The family is the best example of the community. Property is more or less held in common and its distribution is handled not by the price system but a contracted authority. That is why the family cannot be used as an appropriate metaphor for political organization, which relies on the distinctive traits of the state and its monopoly on the legal use of aggressive force.

This difference is not simply one of semantics; it goes to the heart of defining what the classical liberals have called the natural order of liberty. Rights, society, and community are all part of this order. Privileges, politics, and the state—the institutions with which these are usually conflated—are distinct from this natural order of liberty. They are not, of course, entirely separate, but it is essential to understand the difference so that rights do not turn to privileges and become self-devouring. Further, our concept of community has degenerated into warring political interest groups. What is done by political means is confused with what should be done by social means.

To understand the difference requires recognizing the difference between a freely chosen action and an action enforced by coercive edict. There is no need to enter the debate on what precisely constitutes a freely chosen act; the commonsense understanding will suffice: a free act occurs in the absence of an aggressive use of force, coercion of the kind that can be exercised by both private criminals and public officials in their various capacities. A social and economic order dominated by a voluntary exchange matrix, the essence of the business economy, is a free social order. On the other end of the spectrum is the social order dominated by networks of regulators, revenuers, monetary managers, and state social workers. The most extreme form of the latter culminated in the socialist experiment in the Soviet Union and Eastern Europe. These societies were not free in the sense I use the term. Most systems of government today represent a combination of these polar opposites, and much of modern political dialogue consists in conflating the two different philosophies. That does not, however, diminish their usefulness as ideal types—free versus controlled—especially in providing indicators of the appropriate direction of change.

The Social Context of Morality

In the same way that economic liberty lacks a widely accepted moral defense, we are too casual about the liberty of the individual. It is fashionable, of course, in many circles, to defend personal liberties, even when these have been misnamed. The content of the singer's song or a writer's text is often denounced and even censored, but the broadly defined right of free speech is rarely objected to in principle. When it comes to the rights of traders to trade what they wish how they wish, and buyers to buy what they wish in a manner they think right and proper, many people see this as another matter altogether. The objections mount if we speak of the right of businessmen to make as much money as they wish and to accumulate wealth to any extent they wish. Far from being a human right, it is considered to be a right of society to tax them and redistribute their earnings. The degree of vehemence directed at wealth is sometimes qualified by the nature and source of one's earnings (a wealthy physician is sometimes seen as less objectionable than a wealthy stock trader).

Nonetheless, the connection between economic and personal liberty should be clarified. It matters little to writers to be told they have the right to write what they wish if they are not permitted to buy a typewriter or computer, or if they do not have the right to sell their works to anyone who will buy them. Likewise, the freedom to exchange information and to promote one's talents, which is in essence what advertising is, and for that matter what trading itself is, displays the connection between the personal and the economic.

The curtailment of economic liberty leads easily to a curtailment of personal liberty in much the same way that the enhancement of economic liberty may lead to the enhancement of personal liberty, as Milton Friedman has argued.[3] Indeed, a cogent argument can be put forth making the case that a significant reason for the rapid collapse of communism in Eastern Europe had to do with the progress made in economic liberty via communications technology. Computers have made the exchange of information easier, and economic progress became dependent in part on the exchange of information. This made it considerably more difficult for totalitarian regimes to effectively control other means of information, such as political ideas and dissenting opinions.

Rightly understood personal liberty is also tied to the freedom to act based on religious and moral conviction and for those convictions to take on a social dimension. No civilization in history has survived or flourished without a religious foundation. Nor have great classical liberal thinkers neglected the spiritual dimension of man. From the writings of the late Scholastics to eighteenth-century British economists, they have always discovered a link between faith and freedom.

It is an unfortunate consequence of the growing secularism of our time that religion and oppression are two words somehow

---

3   Milton Friedman, *Capitalism and Freedom* (Chicago: University of Chicago Press, 1962).

linked in the public mind. The authentic expression of religious values and high moral principles requires that political oppression be minimized. As F. A. Hayek said:

> Freedom is the matrix required for the growth of moral values—indeed not merely one value among many but the source of all values.... It is only where the individual has choice, and its inherent responsibility, that he has occasion to affirm existing values, to contribute to their further growth, and to earn moral merit.[4]

The term *values* assumes many meanings within the modern political context. Although the word has normative overtones, its technical meaning is simply a ranking, suggesting a subjective preference revealed in thought or action with no inherent moral content. What Hayek is suggesting, however, is that good choices and rightly ordered values can only have a transcendent meaning if freely chosen. Liberty is the source of all values because values cannot have concrete meaning in absence of the freedom to demonstrate them in action. Personal values are variously acquired on the basis of family, culture, religion, personal preference, and the like. What we need is a political and economic system that allows for the free exercise of those values in a manner not inconsistent with the equal right of others to pursue theirs.

Forcing one view of proper values through political means always runs the risk of purging the moral substance of goodness. Can a person be said to be noble or heroic if it were not a freely chosen action on his or her part that displayed either nobility or heroism? Hayek's phrase "earn moral merit" is particularly appropriate because no heroic act is considered as such if compelled by a third party.

---

4 F. A. Hayek, "The Moral Element in Free Enterprise," in *The Spiritual and Moral Significance of Free Enterprise* (New York: National Association of Manufacturers, 1961), 26–27.

It is of course possible and even praiseworthy for people to make moral choices under coercion as an act of resistance, as a martyr accepts death rather than moral compromise. It would, however, be absurd to hold up the ethics of resistance as a guidepost to the right ordering of public life. The relevant question is whether virtue itself can be the product of force. In the authentic sense, it cannot. When freedom is absent from the context of ideals such as morality, nobility, compassion, or heroism, the result is to strip the action of its meritorious component. A morality that is not chosen is no morality at all. Only human beings with volition can be said to be moral, and in order to act in a moral way one must have liberty. Liberty is not so much a virtue by definition as it is the essential social condition that makes virtue possible.

Looked at another way, a close connection exists between the spiritual and physical. These two aspects of the human character are what make up the human reality: human beings are flesh and spirit. We are not like angels, who have no bodies; we are not like beasts, who have no conscience. Animals are bound by instinct; humans are related to things by reason because we are self-reflecting. It is the rational relationship between the human person and nature that gives rise to the desire to assume dominion over the resources given to us by God in the world and to transform them as God transformed nothingness into the physical world at the creation (*ex nihilo*).

What, then, is the appropriate and legitimate use of coercion in social intercourse? It is widely understood that individual physical aggression against person or property is wrong. Difficulties arise when the same moral criterion is extended to society at large. Despite conventional wisdom, wrong does not become right when morally identical acts are committed at the political level by the state. Physical violence against person or property should not be used as an act of aggression in any context; physical violence may, however, be used in defense of the rights of person and property, to enforce restitution for crimes committed, and to satisfy the demands of justice (classically defined as giving to each his due). Everything else in life is best left to the noncoercive sphere where additional and effective norms apply. All of this flows from the principle that voluntary action is more suited to moral action than to coercion. Lord Acton offered this succinct expression of this view of politics: "Liberty is not a means to a higher political end. It is itself the highest political end."

Lord Acton did not argue that personal liberty is itself the highest end of man, which would be a land of hedonism. The land of liberty Acton is upholding is not unrestricted. We are not speaking about free love or free thought. His emphasis is on the political, the sphere in which the distinguishing feature is the legal use of aggressive force. Insofar as we concern ourselves with the proper function of the state, Acton's dictum is correct. Rights are best protected by strictly limiting the state's power to use aggressive force. When the state is used for wealth redistribution, unjust wars, inflation, and confiscatory economic regulation, the state comes up against Acton's dictum about the political order: Its primary purpose is the advancement of liberty. Beyond that, the promotion of virtue is best left to the natural order of liberty, meaning church, family, community, and tradition.

In the same sense that upholding freedom is not sanctioning moral license, neither is liberty inconsistent with rightly exercised authority. "Authority," writes Robert Nisbet, "is rooted in the statutes, functions, and allegiances which are the components of any association—Authority, like power, is a form of constraint, but, unlike power, is based ultimately upon consent of those under it; that is, it is unconditional."[5] It is often thought that the opposite of power is antinomianism, as if anarchy reigns where the state does not interfere. Nisbet is suggesting that a middle ground exists between lawlessness and power, namely the structures of

---

[5] Robert Nisbet, *The Quest for Community: A Study in the Ethics and Order of Freedom* (San Francisco: ICS Press, 1990), xxvi.

authority offered under liberty. The most strict of all legitimate authority is the security of private property, which requires that all property must be initially owned, produced, or contracted for.

The facts of scarcity, human frailty, and original sin are existential realities from which only the kingdom of God can ultimately deliver the human race. Freedom can make no such claim. What freedom can do, indeed what history attests the freedom of exchange has done with remarkable proficiency, is to maximize human resources to their fullest, to the greatest benefit of humankind. As most entrepreneurs realize, the free market functions as a moral tutor by fostering rule-keeping, honesty, respect for others, and bravery. Markets and the entrepreneurs who enable the market to function do this because they require, in the first place, a certain moral context in which to exist and function smoothly. Firms cannot long exist without a reputation for honesty; quality workmanship; and, in most cases, civility and politeness. Given the fact that a free market depends on voluntary exchange to operate, if some of the virtues were lacking, consumers are the best judge of when to end the relationship. In fact, the practical intelligence of the market is its most obvious virtue. It can be seen both by the consumer who is looking for a good deal, as well as by the business person who must be other-regarding by tending to the needs and desires of the consumer. In this respect, the system in which the entrepreneur must operate requires and promotes altruistic behavior, as George Gilder has argued.[6]

In the promotion of traditions, manners, ethics, and virtue, voluntary institutions are more trustworthy than the state, and more effective as well. These matters are too important to be entrusted to bureaucrats and politicians. The opposition here is not to social authority but to unjust coercive power, especially

---

[6] George Gilder, *Spirit of Enterprise* (New York: Simon and Schuster, 1984).

when it becomes centralized. What Nisbet calls intermediary institutions, social arrangements of authority that provide a buffer between the individual and the state, are critically important.

In the development and flourishing of these institutions, private property—in the means of production, distribution, and exchange—is a necessary foundation. Private property and wealth do not exist in a state of nature; they come about when people decide that the creation of a civilized community requires some agreement about what is mine and what is thine. It is not enough to wander from place to place and take from others as the moment calls for. There must be rules of who owns what and what the terms of agreement and exchange will be. The defense of the right of property ownership should not be seen as the defense of detached material objects in themselves, but of the dignity, liberty, and very nature of the human person. The right to own and control justly acquired property is an extension and exercise of authentic human rights.

Religion and Liberty

Religion is, among other things, a social phenomenon—it emerges from human interaction and, at least in part, pertains to the human realm. The question of what standards ought to characterize that interaction, and the extent to which one member of the human community has rights and claims against other members fall within the realm of legitimate religious concerns.

No doubt some would prefer that if religion has to exist at all, it is best confined to an exclusively private sphere. Thus, the doctrine of the separation of church and state is seen as one guarantor of liberty. In today's climate, this doctrine frequently carries with it a placard appeal among those who are hostile to any impression that religion is approved or appreciated in public life. We need not look very far to see the horrors the media expresses when a religious institution is granted tax relief or an ecclesiastical leader is invited to offer an invocation at a public event or a church body stakes out a particular policy position. Even simple prayers in an American public school classroom are taboo for fear that one student in thirty might somehow feel ostracized by a few moments of silence. Indeed the most vociferous contemporary defenders of separation seem bent on constructing an impermeable wall not only between the church and the state but also and primarily between religion and society. In the name of pluralism, some seek to elevate the principle of separation to a sacrosanct maxim motivated by intolerant attitudes.

The irony here is that the true ideal of separation owes its full force and vitality to religious ideas that throughout history have developed the notion of a court of appeal higher than that of the state, and attempt to establish a restriction on the power of the state. The religious concept of man as a free being endowed with certain inalienable rights makes it possible for anyone to assert his or her independence against a leviathan. This concept, moreover, paves the way for mans participation in the commonwealth as a free being capable of exercising rights and privileges that could not be so easily secured in a system lacking a transcendent reference point, as history has so often and so harshly demonstrated.

We cannot deny that some of the most egregious violations of human rights have been committed at the hands of religious leaders who claimed the authority of God to use coercion against heretics, schismatics, and others. Such disregard for political and religious liberty, though, suffers from an internal contradiction. It bespeaks a misunderstanding of creation and the fall, wherein God grants the human family free will, and does so in the face of distinct possibility that wrong choices are possible. An amalgamation of church and state also makes for a very unsure footing when the political constellation is altered so as to place the heretics in charge who then proceed to outlaw orthodoxy, using the political mechanisms that are already in place.

The seeds of liberty were first germinated four thousand years ago among that group of wandering nomads who praised the name of Yahweh. Exodus 1–14 relates the story of oppression of the ancient Israelites by the Egyptians. In their cry for freedom, the children of Israel yearned for more than mere release from their cruel taskmasters. They desired to establish their own domain where the laws of God would act as a means of governance to ensure the necessary liberties for their people. Liberty under the law of Yahweh was the only conceivable liberty the Hebrew people would accept. They knew intuitively that their survival depended on a community bonded together by a singular faith in a creator who in turn bound himself to them by a supernatural covenant.

As long as the people remained faithful to God, they enjoyed a certain liberty in the world, and the Ten Commandments delivered by Moses set the standard by which that liberty was to be exercised. We read the promise of the covenant in Exodus 19:5–7: "If you will indeed obey my voice and keep my covenant, you shall be my treasured possession among all peoples, for all the earth is mine; and you shall be to me a kingdom of priests and a holy nation."

It would be a mistake, however, to think that the Jews established a political arrangement in the sense that surrounding ancient nations did. The particular Hebrew genius consisted in what may be called a religious rule of life whereby the prophets, rabbis, and other leaders kept political leaders in line through wise admonition. The widespread use of religious courts, consisting of elders, to judge individual matters kept the community largely clear of what we would call today state intervention.[7]

---

[7] Meir Tamari, *With All Your Possessions: Jewish Ethics and Economic Life* (New York: The Free Press, 1987).

While it is true that Jewish tradition places a heavy emphasis on the role and authority of the community in individual decisions, there was also introduced into the ancient world in this nascent ideal a respect for individual dignity. We detect a permissible pluralism at this time, as seen in the different expectations of those who were part of the Hebrew convenant, as distinct from those outside of it, yet who sojourned within the Jewish domain.[8]

When considering the Hebrew relationship to any state, two presuppositions must be maintained: God is King and God is the source of justice. The assertion that God is King places ultimate sovereignty outside the human dimension and entails the notion that everyone on earth, including the rulers, are subservient to Him. When any leader disregarded this precept and began to substitute his sovereignty for God's, the Hebrews protested vigorously, recognizing the inherent dignity that each individual has before God and that no one can tread upon this dignity with impunity. The assertion that God is the source of justice enabled the Jewish people to escape tyranny by an appeal to an objective standard of justice against oppression. Such a transcendent belief, either implicitly or explicitly, survives in a society governed by "the rule of law." No society could be held together very long without some kind of higher reference point, lest individuals find themselves vulnerable to the excesses of the stronger against the weaker. We find in the Jews the rudimentary notion that a high morality is a prerequisite for ordered liberty to flourish.

When we look back two thousand years to the center of the civilized world we observe how those seeds sprouted in the Christian idea. From the Christian perspective, the most important events in human history are the incarnation, death, and resurrection of Jesus Christ. These events represent a deepening appreciation in human consciousness of the sacredness of the individual. They happen, after all, to an individual, and for other individuals. In

---

8   Cf. Deuteronomy 14:21.

the last analysis, the purpose of Christ's appearance in human history is to redeem concrete human beings, not abstractions. His teachings are those of the prophet who calls for conversion within the individual heart first, and by extension as though by a leavening process that conversion is extended throughout society. The reverse would be impossible.

The Christian message employs the model of the family, not the state, as the ideal human community. It emphasizes love rather than power as the distinguishing mark of the true believer and the binding force of the community. As Alexander Ruestow observes, "in its doctrine of immortality and of the infinite worth of each human being as a child of God" and "in placing every individual human soul in direct relation to God" Christianity furnished "a strong counterweight to its other components of restraint and conscience." It was this that gave rise to antidomination tendencies and formed the "roots of individualism and liberalism."[9]

Christ's teaching about the celestial kingdom would have wide-ranging political impact. This is seen, for instance, in the radical commitment that the early Christians made to his message, and the way in which the blood of the first Christian martyrs served as a strong reminder of the limited claim of the state over the human heart.

This witness of the martyrs in opposition to the coercive dictates of the state played a major role in eventually converting a sufficient number of political leaders to the faith. Soon the liberty of Christian worship would come to be accepted as a right by pagan society. Likewise, the belief in an afterlife enabled Christians to make sacrifices that the surrounding pagan society came to respect and admire, which in turn called into question the extent of allegiance owed the state.

---

9   Alexander Ruestow, *Freedom and Domination* (Princeton, NJ: Princeton University, 1980), 250.

In the early part of the fourth century, religious liberty came to be tolerated in the Roman Empire. *The Edict of Toleration*, promulgated in 311, demonstrates the shift. "After the publication, on our part, of an order commanding Christians to return to the observance of the ancient customs," said the edict, "many of them, it is true, submitted in view of the danger, while many others suffered death. Nevertheless, since many of them have continued to persist in their opinions—we, with our wonted clemency, have judged it is wise to extend a pardon even to these men and permit them once more to become Christians and re-establish their places of meetings."

What began as an adversarial relationship between Christianity and the state eventually turned into tolerance and finally into acceptance. With Constantine, the church and state were amalgamated as the Roman Empire adopted Christianity. In addition to providing Christianity with certain liberties and advantages, this amalgamation likewise saddled it with a heavy yoke that it would bear until the middle of the twentieth century.

Saint Thomas Aquinas brought the mightiest mind of the Middle Ages to bear on the question of human rights and liberty. By synthesizing Aristotle with Christianity, Saint Thomas developed the theory of natural law, which he described in the following manner:

> Now, among, all others, the rational creature is subject to Divine providence in the most excellent way, in so far as it partakes of a share of providence, by being provident both for itself and for others. Wherefore it has a share of the Eternal Reason, whereby it has a natural inclination to its proper act and end; and this participation of the eternal law in the rational creature is called natural law.[10]

---

[10] *Summa*, I-II, q. 90, art. 2.

Regarding the impact of natural law on human law, Thomas says: "Consequently every human law has just so much of the nature of law, as it is derived from the law of nature."[11]

The resiliency of natural law throughout the centuries is seen in the name of the endeavor. Natural law is resilient because it accounts for and makes sense of reality. The coherence of natural law is twofold: It coheres with experience and with reason. It establishes a reference point, as did the Law and the Prophets for the Jews outside of institutional dictate. Most importantly for the development of liberty and especially economic liberty, it establishes the sanctity of the individual as a rational being who can interpret the relationship between the individual and the community in terms of free association and contract.

Emerging from this concept of human beings as free persons, autonomous yet in relation to one another, the disciples of Saint Thomas went on to apply their moral theory and deductive methodology to the realm of economics. In a systematic sense, these scholars, the late Scholastics, founded the discipline of economics long before the time of Adam Smith.[12] In his massive treatise on the history of economic thought, Joseph Schumpeter writes: "It is within their system of moral theology and the law that economics gained definite if not separate existence, and it is they who come nearer than does any other group to having been the founders of scientific economics."[13]

A comparison of the thinking of many of these medieval Scholastics on economic liberty with modern free-market proponents reveals an astonishing harmony.[14] The similarities begin

---

[11] *Summa*, I-II, q. 95, art. 2.

[12] See Alejandro A. Chafuen, *Faith and Liberty: The Economic Thought of the Late Scholastics* (Lanham, MD: Lexington Books, 2003).

[13] Joseph Schumpeter, *History of Economic Analysis* (New York: Oxford University Press, 1954), 97.

[14] Chafuen, *Faith and Liberty*.

at the justification of property and exchange, continue through the analysis of value and economic growth, and extend all the way to money, banking, and the theory of interest rates. Even the analysis of taxation and regulation bears a striking similarity, given the many centuries that separate modern free-market thought from these disciples of Saint Thomas.

Centesimus Annus, the 1991 encyclical of Pope John Paul II, recaptures the Scholastic economic tradition for modern Christians. Exactly what the pope's economic influences were in preparing the encyclical are impossible to determine. Prior to the promulgation of the document, the Vatican met with a series of mainstream Western economists, among them Kenneth Arrow, Hirofumi Uzawa, Anthony Atkinson, Jeffrey Sachs, Hendrick Houthakker, Amartya Sen, Robert Lucas, and Edmund Malinvaud. Their influence is far less evident than the schools representing a more explicitly free-market brand of economic thought, for example, the monetarist, supply-side, public choice, and Austrian schools of modern economics.

In general these latter schools argue that the free-market economy is a process of discovery that carefully balances the scarcity of the world's resources with unlimited demands of consumers and that the free-market mechanism is superior to any alternative in performing this task. They regard the pursuit of private interest, in the context of freedom of contract and private property, as serving both individual good and the good of society as a whole; as a corollary, they do not overlook the private interests of individuals in the state sector and regard them as largely destructive social forces. The allocation of resources, they argue, should be taken care of by the price system because it is more reliable than government macroeconomic management.

*Centesimus Annu*s echoes these themes in many passages. The occasion of the encyclical was the one-hundredth anniversary of *Rerurn Novarum*, but the collapse of socialist central planning in Eastern Europe, what the pope calls the "events of 1989," is also placed at the center of the document. The pope displays a profoundly correct understanding of the importance of the division of labor. He points out that "goods cannot be adequately produced through the work of an isolated individual; they require the cooperation of many people in working towards a common goal." To coordinate the division of labor requires "initiative and entrepreneurial ability."[15] He correctly says that, while not everything man needs is provided through economics, "the free market is the most efficient instrument for utilizing resources and effectively responding to needs."[16]

The word *profit* is not used derisively in his text: "The Church acknowledges the legitimate role of profit as an indication that a business is functioning well. When a firm makes a profit, this means that productive factors have been properly employed and corresponding human needs have been duly satisfied."[17] He has recognized the distinctively human part of the calculation process, and the glory of markets in that they can both satisfy individual interest as well as that of the entire community. The profit is a measure of that satisfaction.

On the development of the Third World, he especially calls for a "breakdown" of "barriers of monopolies which leave so many countries on the margins of development," thus correctly realizing the primary problem of less-developed countries.

> Can it perhaps be said that, after the failure of Communism, capitalism is the victorious social system, and that capitalism should be the goal of the countries now making efforts to rebuild their economy and society? Is this the model which ought to be proposed to the countries of the Third World which are searching for the path to true economic and civil progress?

---

[15] *Encyclical Letter* Centesimus Annus *of the Supreme Pontiff John Paul II on the Hundredth Anniversary of* Rerum Novarum, 1991, par. 32.

[16] *Encyclical Letter* Centesimus Annus, par. 34.

[17] *Encyclical Letter* Centesimus Annus, par. 35.

The pope says yes, if by capitalism we mean "an economic system which recognizes the fundamental and positive role of business, the market, private property and the resulting responsibility for the means of production, as well as free human creativity in the economic sector."[18]

The religious concept of God's creation of the human family in his own image, and hence with an intrinsic dignity, has made a significant contribution to the modern understanding of the limitations of power in social and political relationships, as well as the need for human beings to enjoy legitimate autonomy. Political and economic liberty is misunderstood, however, if it is seen as resulting in a completely secularized and libertine society, or if it entails the notion that citizens animated by religious ideals may not be permitted to have an impact on their communities. Political liberty does not demand theological or moral relativism. It merely guarantees that moral and religious ends are not achieved by political means, that is, coerced by the state.

The process of extracting the church from the direct responsibility of ordering the political arrangements of each country to a religious end has been a long and arduous one, and is not completely finished. John Courtney Murray, the American Jesuit whose work on religious liberty and American pluralism contributed greatly to the doctrinal development in the Catholic Church's understanding of religious freedom as a human right, said, "in all honesty it must be admitted that the church is late in acknowledging the validity of the principle."[19]

Yet the theme of immunity from coercion is picked up in *Dignitatis Humanae*, the Vatican II document on religious liberty, which outlines a legitimate sphere of political liberty with-

---

[18] *Encyclical Letter* Centesimus Annus, par. 42.

[19] John Courtney Murray, "Contemporary Orientation of Catholic Thought on Church and State in the Light of History," *Theological Studies* 10 (June 1949): 181.

out compromising the truth-claims of the Christian faith. The document draws the following distinction: "This sacred Synod likewise professes its belief that it is upon the human conscience that these obligations [to seek truth] fall and exert their binding force. The truth cannot impose itself except by virtue of its own truth, as it makes its entrance into the mind at once quietly and with power."[20]

Perhaps the greatest example of an organized political system of intolerance that both religious and secular societies have had to endure was that of centrally planned socialism, but this should not surprise us. It is consistent for a regime that believes it can plan the entire economy, which means to dictate the economic decisions of every citizen, to find little room in society for religious freedom. By attempting to own and control private property, and to suppress religious and political expression and the freedom of association, the totalitarian rulers of Central and Eastern Europe hoped to produce a society sanitized of any reference to God.

Certainly many factors went into the astounding and rapid demise of communism, but it would be an oversight to neglect the role of religion—Catholic, Protestant, and Jewish—in finally undermining the illegitimate authority the state had claimed for itself. It would also be an oversight to neglect the role of religion in providing a secure moral foundation for freedom so that liberty may be used properly and defended in moral terms. The contributions of religion to the development of the free society and the further implications for our future understanding of political liberty have only begun to be explored.

Entrepreneurship and the Welfare State

Having defined the terms of the debate, presented the view that freedom is an essential condition for the exercise of virtue, and

[20] Documents of the Second Vatican Council, *Declaration on Religious Freedom* (Dignitatis Humanae), par. 1.

traced the religious foundations of liberty, a discussion of two modern institutions should help clarify the principles of liberty. Those institutions are entrepreneurship, which rests on voluntarism and creativity, and the welfare state, which rests on state interventionism. The current moral terminology used to discuss and evaluate the two institutions is gravely deficient and in need of radical corrections.

The experience of totalitarian societies has taught us the need to be wary of the power of the state and to be more tolerant of what is often called "diversity." The word *diversity* also implies recognition that there are differences between people. While we may all labor under the same rules, the kind of work we do and what we produce will differ according to our different temperaments and talents. In economic thought, the resulting matrix of individual differences is called the division of labor.

It is an unfortunate holdover of old socialist notions that the religious community is not yet entirely comfortable with the concept of the division of labor. Religious leaders are not prepared to grant that all economic actors can also be moral beings. The capitalist is not given the same moral status as the laborer, for example. The person who lives off investment income is not considered as morally upright as the wage earner, and the replacement worker is not considered as virtuous as the striker. Yet all this is confusion. If a person is using his or her talents in a peaceful manner, if an assumed position in the division of labor does not conflict with moral teaching, there is no reason to condemn any occupation. In the free market, all persons occupy a position in the economy according to individual strengths and all can use their respective positions to good or ill.

With few exceptions, the religious establishment views entrepreneurs (people whose profession requires risking scarce capital in markets to create future goods and services) as one of the least favored groups in society. One sees evidence of the prejudice against the entrepreneur everywhere. Books, television programs, films, cartoon strips, and sermons all convey the same message: what he does is rapacious, greedy, and socially destructive. Business may be a necessary evil, says reigning opinion, but the entrepreneur should never be given a moral sanction. That is conventional wisdom as proclaimed by the opinion-molding classes.

This fundamentally reflects a bias against capitalism, and has spiritual consequences. As a priest, I often find entrepreneurs who are disenfranchised and alienated from their churches. All they hear from their churches is that the path to personal redemption is to give up all their money. Some religious leaders, however, display very little understanding of the vocation called entrepreneurship, of what it requires in the way of personal sacrifice, and of what it contributes to society. In virtually all the seminaries with which I am acquainted there is no course on economics; that, unfortunately, has not kept religious leaders from pronouncing on economic matters.

In addition, the lack of understanding most often comes from people who operate from a distributivist economic model. On Sunday morning a collection basket is passed. On Monday the bills are paid and acts of charity are attended to. If the money is short, they appeal for more. There is nothing wrong with this model, but it tends to foster a view of the economic world as a pie that needs to be divided. Those who take a large piece are forcing small pieces on others. The entrepreneur operates on an entirely different model. He or she talks of making money, not collecting it; of producing, not redistributing, wealth. He or she must consider the needs, wants, and desires of consumers because the only way to get money peacefully and without charity is to offer something of value in exchange.

A more proper economic analysis teaches that entrepreneurs are impresarios, visionaries who organize numerous factors, take risks, and bring resources into connection with each other to create something greater than the sum of the parts. They drive the economy forward by anticipating the wishes of the public and creating new ways of organizing resources.[21] They are the men and women who create jobs, reduce human suffering, discover and apply new cures, bring food to those without, and help dreams become realities. This creative aspect of the entrepreneur is akin to God's creative activity as it appears in the book of Genesis (as Michael Novak has argued). In order to carry out this creative enterprise, entrepreneurs must have access to the material factors of production; they must be permitted to acquire and trade property. They must act in an atmosphere of freedom. They should not have to suffer slights from religious leaders who do not approve of talents and gifts God has given them. Does this elevate the entrepreneurial technique above the spiritual dimension of man? Not at all, as Etienne Gilson put it, "technique is that without which the most fervent piety is powerless to make use of nature for Gods sake."[22]

What is ultimately extraordinary about the institution of entrepreneurship is that it requires no third-party intervention to make it come into being and thrive. It requires no government program or government manuals. It does not require special low-interest loans, special tax treatment, or public subsidies. It does not require a specialized education or prestigious degree. Entrepreneurship is an institution that grows organically from the natural order of liberty. Those with talent, even the calling, toward economic creativity are compelled by nature to enter it and lead society in the creation of wealth.

What does this call mean to those in the vocation of enterprise? It means that they must strive to be more fully what they are, to display more fully the virtue of inventiveness, to act more boldly

---

[21] See Joseph Schumpeter, *The Theory of Economic Development* (Cambridge: Harvard University Press, 1949).

[22] Etienne Gilson, "L'intelligence au service du Christ-Roi," in *Christianisme et Philosophie* (Paris: J. Vrin, 1936), 155–56.

with the virtue of creativity, to continue to be other-regarding as they anticipate market demands, as they develop in themselves and school others in the virtue of thrift. They should not merely share their wealth with those in need but also act as tutors to others by example and mentorship. They must teach others to become independent and to produce wealth themselves.

Truly, the gifts that entrepreneurs offer society at large are beyond anything they themselves and others can completely comprehend. The entrepreneur is the source of more social and spiritual good than is recognized. In contrast, the welfare state is too often thought of in morally favorable terms, but its social consequences, however well intended, can be largely damaging.

For decades, the provider state has been thought to be an effective compromise between the oppression of full-blown socialism and the alleged uncertainties and rigors of free markets. This provider state offers a variety of extra-market provisions of goods and services. Today, people of many different political stripes agree that the present welfare system does not work. The consensus for radical reform is growing. Yet public representatives of religious bodies and institutions have proved largely unable to adjust to the modern realities of the social welfare state. Sincere and well-thought-out plans to change the incentives of a program or cut government welfare spending—even when it would thereby leave more money for private charities—are often denounced as lacking compassion and even being ill-intended.

The moral high ground on this question is entirely occupied by defenders of welfare redistribution—on the fairly crude premise that Christian charity and coercive wealth transfers are morally identical. Of course Christians have a moral obligation to minister to the poor, for what we do to the least of Christ's brethren, we do to Christ himself. Church leaders, however, have too often conflated Christian duty to help the poor with a supposed moral duty to support the Leviathan enterprise we call the welfare state.

Far from ameliorating poverty, many of these programs have the perverse effect of further subsidizing the initial conditions of eligibility—whether single motherhood, poverty, homelessness, or joblessness. Thus, they create and further the conditions they profess to cure. They foster a debilitating sense of dependency. Religious traditions have always stressed the centrality of the family, yet there is no more effective an opponent of marriage and the family than a government bureaucracy that provides financial incentives against getting married and establishing a family. In many cases, the welfare state has decreased the sense of marital obligation and eroded the values that sustain families. When the state provides for the old and the young, it takes away moral responsibilities from people in the prime of their lives to administer charity to their families. Without such responsibilities, people can too easily fall into consumerism, precisely the condition anticapitalists profess to oppose.

When religious people think about poverty, it is too often in materialist terms. The problem of poverty is not so much one of poor people getting material assistance, it is a problem of establishing human bonding. Marvin Olasky, in his challenging book *The Tragedy of American Compassion*, reminds us that compassion means to suffer with another.[23] Bureaucratized compassion becomes simply giving to another and that tends to create depersonalized dependence. What we need instead is a greater sense of bonding with those who are in need. In this way, we provide role models and incentives for those who want to find their way out of economic deprivation.

Some say that economic redistributionism is a matter of social justice. Yet, if all social relations are based merely on a state-enforced vision of justice, the virtues of love and compassion lose their meaning. Charity is supposed to represent obedience to the

---

[23] Marvin Olasky, *The Tragedy of American Compassion* (Washington, DC: Regnery Gateway, 1992).

dictates of conscience; its character changes when it disintegrates into simple obedience to government agencies.

There are other dangers that priests, rabbis, and ministers face in promoting the government as the resource of first resort. They reduce the incentive of people in the pews to become personally involved in needed projects. People in the pews might think: Why do I need to get involved in helping people who are suffering, feeding the poor, or caring for my neighbor? There is nothing wrong with churches involving themselves in political activities, and, indeed, sometimes religious people must enter political battles out of moral obligation. Regardless, the church's mission should not be relegated to the role of lobbyist; that deprives the church of the spiritual nourishment that comes from actually performing acts of mercy. Political activity also implies a moral obligation to be informed about economics and the consequences of certain kinds of statist policies.

We must wisely consider the most appropriate ways in which our obligations to the poor are carried out. From the earliest Christian reflection on aid to those in need, this obligation was never an unconditional one. While Saint Paul encouraged the early Christian community to remember those in need, he was also prudent and realistic. "If anyone is not willing to work," he said, "let him not eat."[24] Christianity insists on love as a fundamental virtue; but it never advanced the notion that we must subsidize those who can, but refuse to be responsible for their own lives.

The modern welfare state is simply incapable of making the kinds of distinctions that Saint Paul insists are necessary in administering charity. The centralized state, by its nature, administers programs on the assumption that people are identical and that they can be shaped according to an inflexible central plan. Private charity may not be able to do all the work that is necessary, but where and when it is allowed to work, it does a better

---

[24] 2 Thessalonians 3:10.

job than the public sector. It is also based on the principle of voluntary action, as opposed to state coercion, which gives it a morally superior status.

In *Centesimus Annus*, Pope John Paul II expressed reservations about the welfare state, especially the modern one that tries to provide cradle-to-grave public support. "Malfunctions and defects in the Social Assistance State are the result of an inadequate understanding of the tasks proper to the State," he writes. The alternative principle he advances is the notion of subsidiarity: "A community of a higher order should not interfere in the internal life of a community of a lower order, depriving the latter of its functions."[25]

Americans are mostly unfamiliar with the term, much less the substance of, the subsidiarity principle. Europeans know it well but in the context of the debate surrounding the power of the European Union. In that debate, the subsidiarity principle is supposed to serve as public reassurance that the EU bureaucracies in Brussels will not interfere in the affairs of national states when it is not necessary. (It has taken on special meaning with regard to central banking and monetary policy.) The downside of viewing the term in this context is the implication that subsidiarity is about relations among different levels of government. This is far from the case. It is instead about relations among all spheres of life. The first units in society are individuals. They own property and they form families. These families form communities, and communities group together in localities. The circles of authority expand to the state, the region, and the nation. Each circle has its own form of government.

The subsidiarity principle tells us that lower orders ought to perform social functions when they can. Only when failure is evident and it has been thoroughly established that shifting to higher orders would result in an actual improvement should

---

[25] *Centesimus Annus*, par. 48.

functions undergo a transfer. The modern central state has assumed responsibilities not only when it cannot undertake them in a better fashion than lower orders but also when the failures of lower orders are not even evident.

The principle is thus much more widely applicable than the debate over subsidiarity in Europe suggests. The issue is not which government we should trust to take care of us; the issue is that it points to a mandate for decentralizing economic and political functions from the center to the local and individual levels. Here are the principles: (1) property owners should be the producers of first resort, (2) families are the primary government, and (3) local politics is apt to be more consistent with community concerns than distant bureaucracies. This is the way subsidiarity works itself out in a social and normative sense.

What does the principle of subsidiarity imply we do about the poor? "It would appear," says the pope, "that needs are best understood and satisfied by people who are closest to them and who act as neighbors to those in need."[26] This matches our daily experience. If a family member is in trouble, the family has the first responsibility to help. The family member also *wants* to help and knows best *how* to help. The same is true of the relevant community and locality. People throw themselves most fully into projects closest to home where they can monitor the way resources are used and even view the results.

We have learned that government employees do not have the incentive or knowledge to deal with problems of poverty all over vast masses of land and population. It is absurd for the central government to have presumed to undertake such a job. It is as implausible as socialism itself, under which government mandated five-year-production plans and fixed every price. The experiences and lessons that surround the history of socialism are very similar to the ones the welfare state is teaching us today. No one group

[26] *Centesimus Annus*, par. 48.

of planners, no matter how wise and sensitive to human needs they may be, can see the deepest needs of the human soul, which are so frequently at the root of economic problems.

Central planning boards—whether in a Politburo or the various ministries of modern Western governments—rarely improve society and most often interfere with the public's ability to uncover relevant knowledge about local circumstances to address them efficiently. If they were partially deprived of the power and funds to administer poverty programs, resources and capital would be freed to solve local problems locally. The time has come for religious leaders to abandon the mantra of more and more government programs. Instead of erecting more bureaucracies, they should take back from the state their rightful positions as the primary ministers of the welfare of the poor.

Conclusion

Far from having achieved victory, the economic order of liberty is in a precarious position. It is, moreover, entirely evident that in this debate on the morality of economic systems, the advocates of the market economy do not yet have the upper hand. Too often, economists refuse to speak in normative terms, and they often act as if they should not. Those who are charged with pronouncing on morality in public life do not have strong sympathies with the ethic of capitalism—if they are sympathetic with it at all. Most people are content to settle with a system that seems to reconcile the "ethics" of socialism with the productivity of capitalism.

Yet, political economy and ethics should be and must be reconciled. If we continue to promote an "ethics" of socialism, it will eventually endanger institutions that support the productive capacity of capitalism. It is not a trivial fact that every step away from the free market is a step away from voluntarism, and every step toward interventionism is a step away from liberty. It speaks to the essence of what it means to act virtuously.

A moral argument for economic liberty should not shrink from its own logical implications, however politically unfashionable. An imperative against theft and in favor of the security of private property must also suggest caution about taxes above the minimal necessary for the rule of law. Freedom of contract must include the freedom not to contract. Freedom of association must include the freedom not to associate. Toleration of individual differences must include tolerances for the inequality in wealth that will be the unavoidable result. A morality that favors virtue in the context of liberty must allow room for personal moral failure and an understanding of the difference between vice and crime.

It is sometimes said that no one dreams of capitalism. This, too, must change. Rightly understood, capitalism is simply the name for the economic component of the natural order of liberty. It means expansive ownership of property, fair and equal rules for all, economic security through prosperity, strict adherence to the boundaries of ownership, opportunity for charity, wise resource use, creativity, growth, development, prosperity, and abundance. Most of all it means the economic application of the principle that every human person has dignity and should have that dignity respected, it is a dream worthy of our spiritual imaginations.

About the Authors

Reverend Edmund A. Opitz (1914–2006) was a Congregationalist minister and author of the book *Religion and Capitalism: Allies, Not Enemies.* He also served as a member of the senior staff of The Foundation for Economic Education and was a contributing editor of *The Freeman.*

Robert A. Sirico has been active in public policy concerns for over fifteen years. His concern that religious communities today know little about the fundamental economic issues behind today's social problems prompted him to found the Acton Institute for the Study of Religion and Liberty, Grand Rapids, Michigan, in 1990. In addition to undergraduate study at the University of Southern California and the University of London, he received his Master of Divinity degree from the Catholic University of America, and he was ordained a priest in 1989. His pastoral ministry has included a chaplaincy to AIDS patients at the National Institute of Health as well as various parish appointments.

Father Sirico's writings on religious, political, economic, and social matters have been published in a variety of journals in the United States, Latin America, and Europe.